A CRAZY LOVE AFFAIR

(They are so not meant to be together)

By

LAURA HOOKE

Table of content

Synopsis

• the reality or state of being dependent
to a specific substance, thing, or
movement.
• commitment to, devotion to, fixation
with, captivation by, enthusiasm for, affection
of, craziness for, oppression to
All that in my life had nearly
become daily practice, similar to my life was a
long,
never-ending propensity. That was until I met
Stacy Greene. She was delightful and
brimming with life, she was all that I could
at any point request, with one exceptionher
brunette hair. I looked past her hair
variety since she was awesome, in each
other perspective. She was the young lady any
person
can fantasy about having and I'm respected to
have been the person she picked. She
was mine and I was hers. I never
needed to hurt her or make her extremely upset

yet, my life comprised of me needing control, and that was our loophole.

Chapter 1

Sex moves me along ordinary. I awaken considering sex, and I fall asleep reasoning of sex. All over the course of the day I'm considering fucking somebody. It's simply normal to consider sex. My primary care physician says to consider sex is sound perhaps not however much I truly do but sex itself is healthy

The main time I disapprove of my way of behaving is around evening time when I start to lament my activities. However at that point I deal with it and do a similar definite thing the following day. I don't move beyond this, I don't significantly alter my methodologies. I mean I've attempted previously however nothing has at any point worked for me. I will always be an unquenchable fiend.

The most terrible piece of my night other than when the night's end is the point at which the young lady needs to "have a special interaction and get to know one another." I don't do connections. I was never keen on being with

only one individual. I have concluded I will save myself from the future wretchedness, by not getting connected to any lady ever. That is the reason I screw them then leave them.
I know Im going to be a lonely, rich
guy who fucks his life away, but I'd
rather that then waste my time falling
in love with someone when it's just
going to end. The pain of losing the one
you love, isn't worth it to me. Why go
through all of that when I can stay far
away from it. And that's what I plan to
do. Stay far away from love.
I pushed her body in a difficult spot, her hands stuck up, our lips never disengaging regardless of how much air we really wanted. I unfastened her dress and it tumbled down swimming at her lower legs. She rapidly unfastens my pants yet couldn't get them down as far as possible. "They're excessively close." She whimpers prior to surrendering and removing her own bra and undies.

I lament wearing tight pants in circumstances like this yet that never prevents me from putting tight pants on the following day. I pull my pants off and push her to the bed. I go after a condom from the night stand and slip it on prior to removing my fighters and sliding into her.

This is the very thing I anticipate consistently. Regardless of how poop my day was or the way that drained I am, fucking helps me.

She moaned, as I moved all through her at a fast speed. The grating causing me to feel invigorated.

I handle her huge phony bosom in my grasp pulling and pulling on her areola between my thumb and forefingers. She groans as I drove myself more profound into her.

For my purposes, it's not just about the sex. Sure the sex is perfect, however there's something else entirely to it. I have all of the control in circumstances like this. I control who I bring back, how the entire trial goes down, what positions we do, and when she leaves. I never let a young lady start to lead the pack.

"Steve . . . I'm going . . . to come." Her annoyingly piercing voice sounds. When I got her tranquil, she wasn't downright awful.

I clutched the headboard propelling myself more profound within her, our hips slamming into each push.

The vast majority could believe I'm a man prostitute since I screw a great deal of ladies. I realize individuals feel that since I think exactly the same thing. I at times wish I didn't need to be like this. Like one day I will actually want to get by without expecting to have intercourse with somebody.

Each experience just fulfills me for the present, when it's over I'm not generally fulfilled and I need no, I want more.

"In the event that we could do this consistently,"
she panted. I could groan as I delivered, the
come streaming within the condom. I rested my
head in her neck from fatigue.
"Oh my god," She pants trying to
recollect her breath, "That was
amazing. We should do this again
sometime."
I pull myself out of her and toss the
condom in the bin before grabbing my
boxers from the floor.
"Il call you sometime." I lied.
One thing I don't do is give the girl my
number. They don't stop calling and
I don't need them anymore once I'm
done with them. I noticed her getting
comfortable in my bed. "Im sorry to do
this to you, but you have to leave."
"What, you engage in sexual relations with me
then
throw me out?" She sits up on my bed.
"You thought I planned to allow you to remain
in my home since you let me
screw you?" I let out an unpleasant chuckle.

"I'm not leaving. What's more, I'm
tipsy." She folds her arms over her
exposed chest.
"You're level-sufficiently headed. There's a vehicle
outside you can take. Tell him your
address and he will take you there." I
told her.
"That is no joke." she sneers getting up
also, returning her garments on. She
Swore under her breath
telling me I'm "a cold-hearted asshole
who won't ever find love."
I stand from the bed going to the
kitchen to get a bottle of water before
heading off to get a quick rest.

Chapter 2

"We should get a few bitches!" Evan
says air drumming to the beginner
music playing from the radio. I may
be a poop hole, yet Evan. That's is as well's
how we get on sO well. The distinction
among Evan and myself is I would
never call a young lady any such thing.
The term is debasing and very
honestly a very idiotic name to
call somebody. I get called 1,000
names in the book toward one's end
night, yet I don't attempt to return the
disgusting language. Furthermore, for the most
part what they say regarding me is valid. I
am a butt hole, a jerk who just cares
for himself's purposes, a douche with a ton
of cash who generally gets everything he could
possibly want,
sincerely screwed up. I definitely know
things about me, so their words mean
nothing to me.

Evan demanded driving me to the bar rather than
simply meeting me there. I
simply consented to it since I know he
crap confronted he gets when he's alcoholic
furthermore, when I pass on he's compelled to
call a
taxi or to return home with whomever can
track down somebody as revoltingly put
as him alluring. When I get a young lady for
the evening, I leave him precisely where
he is. Furthermore, the following day, he whines
about me being a horrendous companion. He's
fortunate he even has a companion like me
that is willing drives him around like a
escort.
"Steve, would you say you are paying attention
to me?"
He hits my arms taking me from my
contemplations.
"No." I answer honestly. "What were
you saying?"
"I realize brunettes aren't your sort, yet
the previous evening I saw this wonderful
brunette

ogling at you throughout the evening."
"Recently?" I returned home with a
blonde, I didn't see a brunette
gazing at me yesterday.
As terrible as this might sound, I attempt to
keep away from brunettes at all expense. There
are an excessive number of things about them
that
help me to remember old, revolting
recollections.
For one's purposes, my fantasy. At the point
when I initially began
having that bad dream, I've attempted to
avoid brunette's by and large. Which didn't work
since bunches of ladies from my last were
brunette.
"Better believe it, I would've went dependent
upon her to take
her for myself yet she was gazing at
you so hard, I would have rather not intruded."
He says giggling.
"You sure she was certainly not a blonde? You
know how you get when you're
shitfaced."

"Actually..." he stops briefly, "I
had very strong suspicions she had earthy
colored hair,
in any case, you could be correct." He shrugs.
I transform into the part of the bar and we
hustle inside. Who's getting back home
with me this evening? I examine around the
place searching for anybody I could
see as somewhat alluring. There were
ladies all over the place, it was like picking
frozen yogurt from the frozen yogurt shop. So
a wide range of flavors to look over,
vanilla, chocolate, caramel, strawberry,
Oreo
"Steve!" I heard an old, old school
companion, Robert, shout to me. Make
sure to put additional accentuation on the
word old. It's been a very long time since I've
seen him not to mention conversed with him.
The
man that I used to be well actually am
made a poop hole move and demolished our
kinship. However I imagined I didn't
care that we were no longer companions,

I did really partake in the time I once
enjoyed with him. I push past the bodies
in the bar advancing toward him.
"Crap Steve! I didn't realize you were
coming."
"I'm dependably here, it's unique
seeing you around once more." When we
were companions, going out to bars and
clubs weren't exactly his thing.
He simply needed to zero in on his specialty
furthermore, said I was diverting him from
what meant quite a bit to him. He was
a hopeful craftsman when we were in
school together. I couldn't say whether he of all
time
followed his fantasy about selling his specialty,
in spite of everything that I said to him I realized
he was
great at what he did.
He directs his concentration toward the young
lady on
his right. As she converses with him, I had a go
at envisioning her without all the garments.
She is totally gorgeous; her face,

her thrilling edge. Other than her brunette
hair, she was the very sort of
Lady I would need to see stripped. Furthermore,
as far as I could tell, she was coming
home with me this evening. "She's with
you?" I ask him once she strolls over to
the bar.
She was watching me watch her,
prodding me as I talked with Robert
thinking about every one of the manners in
which I could fuck
her this evening. My fingers jerking at my
sides as she shakes her hips quietly to
the music playing around us.
"Her?" He focuses his thumb in her
heading. "No. Well indeed, however no.""What
does that mean?"
"I brought her here, however we're not
together or anything. She's simply a
companion." She investigates her shoulder at
me giving me that look, and there's nothing more
to it
I really want to realize she needs me. I give

Robert a well disposed pat on his back previously
going to take my most memorable action.
I sit straightforwardly close to her, "What's your name?"
"Stacy." She grins, she seems as though she
needs to say something different yet she
rules against it.
"Well you're lovely, stacy."She becomes
flushed, "Wonderful, yourself."
"Hello!" I get the barkeeps consideration.
"Get her one more of what she's
"No," she protests. "I needn't bother with
any longer." She calls attention to her full
glass of anything that reasonable fluid she was
drinking.
I get her cup, she gazes at me
shocked and I sneer and taste it to see
what she's drinking. "Water truly?
Who goes to a bar and doesn't drink?"
"You." I can as of now tell she jumps at the
chance to
put on a show. In any case, who doesn't cherish a
challenge. "I don't drink."

"Who goes to a bar and doesn't drink?"
She taunts my past assertion. "I
try not to drink all things considered."
"So what are you doing here?" I question.
"A similar explanation you're here." Better
believe it,
being her is most certainly going. "What's
your name?"
"Steve."
"All things considered, meeting you Steve is
great. Do
you need to leave?" Screw yes.

Chapter 3

When we returned to my home, she
glanced around and got on her telephone,
not giving me any consideration. However, I
watched her intently.
Her face was delightful due to her
creativity, she doesn't look like the
larger part of the ladies around here.
Her figure was considerably more flawless.
Likely the most surprising thing
about her was the way her body
bended and the astonishing state of
her skin. Her skin just looked delicate and
solid, with a genuine tan, not the phony
splash tans you as a rule find around here.
She hada tasteful feel to the way she
strolled, she clearly thought often about the
way she looked. Nonetheless, you could
tell she had a filthy side. She doesn't actually
look scandalous by any means, yet she
absolutely has
seen a man or two. She was essentially a
D cup and she wouldn't hesitate to draw
consideration them, which is effectively the

hottest piece of her body. He legs were
thin, areas of strength for however, kind of legs
that
are asking to be seen under a short
dress ora skirt. Yet, she wore pants and
her behind fit totally in them.
She at long last sits on the calfskin sofa
at the point when she was finished looking
around.
"Three things before we do anything." I
start and she slants her head aside,
in a confounded at this point entertained manner.
"To start with,
try not to hope to see me again after this.
Two, don't return here, on the grounds that
my security won't ever give you access. Also,
finally, anything you do, don't fall in
love with me."
She gestures and grins, "We meet for five
minutes and you consequently anticipate that I
should become hopelessly enamored with you?
How presumptuous
could you at any point be?"
"I simply end up affecting

Ladies."
"I bet you do mister superstar. This is a
pleasant spot you have here."
"Could we avoid the entirety of the gab
furthermore, get to the genuine justification for
why we came
here."
I hurry on the Lounge chair close to her and
hurriedly interfacing our lips. She pulls
back from the get go yet I place my arm around
her back holding her set up and she
kissed back. Our lips embellishment to one
another's like we've been doing this
for some time. She pushes me down on
the love seat starting to lead the pack and I let
her.
Why? I have no fucking sign.
She rides my lap and sends me
a puerile smile as she unfastens my
pants. I planned to take her shirt off
in any case, I was diverted once she put
her hand over my fighters, on top of my
developing erection. She gradually moves
her hand all over provoking me.

I pull her down to me and associating
our lips once more. My tongue pushing past her
lips and kneading hers. We brealk
the kiss for much required air and she
chomps the skin on my ear. Causing the
blood in my body to rush directly to my
crotch. "Go... quicker."
She does similarly as I say and I take off
the bra from under her shirt. I felt the
goosebumps ascend on her skin as I did as such.
After I got her bra off, I put my hand
under her shirt to grasp a her
bosom once more. She inclines down, pushing
her bosom into my hands and kisses
me. I daintily squeeze her areolas and she
groans into my mouth.
She grasps her hand from my jeans just
as I was going to come. She gradually pulls
my hands from her shirt, my fingers
run down her midsection, and she stands up and
puts her shoes on.
"Where are you going?
"I have activities." She gets her
bra and places it in her sack. No, this

isn't occurring. She giggles, "Jesus
Steve, I genuinely want to believe that you didn't
think I was
going to engage in sexual relations with you."
"For what other reason did you think I brought
you
here?" I question, outrage developing inside
of me.
Once more, she giggles, "Have a goodbye
Steve. I'll see you around at some point."
She winks at me as she leaves
the entryway, and I needed to call Linda to
complete her
incomplete work.

Linda asked me what I was
going to do about Stacy. Linda knows
I can't deal with being turned down or
driven on and nothing occurs, it irritates
me until I take care of business. This
hasn't occurred to me in some time-
entirely. Also, I certain as damnation will not
allow her to get off that simple.
"What's the young lady's number?" I inquires

Evan who was sat on my love seat eating
food from my refrigerator. We talk once later
a couple of years and out of nowhere we're
companions
once more and he can just come to my
house and act Cool with me.
"What young lady?" He bites upsettingly
boisterous.
"Stacy, your companion from the previous
evening." I rub the sides of my sanctuary,
attempting to
disregard his uproarious biting.
"Gracious, why, you succumbing to her?" He
inquires
giggling with a significant piece. Awful.
"Evan, I lack the capacity to deal with your
questions." I bark at him, irritated by
his presence, his biting, and just him
overall. "Simply give me her number so
I can take her out, also, keep all of your
question and remarks to yourself."
"Chill, you don't get to fuck a
young lady once and out of nowhere that is no
joke."

"How would you realize I didn't screw her?"
He disregards me murmuring, "This is
just a burden," prior to giving me her number.

He disregards me murmuring, "This is just a
burden," prior to giving me her number.

"Hi?" She replied.

"You recollect me, don't you Stacy?"

"How in the world did you get my number?"
Despite the fact that I can't see her, I know she's
sneering.

"Go out with me this evening." I say overlooking
her inquiry.

"No, would you say you are joking? I never gave
you my number." She says snickering. Each time
she says no, I get irritated and furthermore
energized realizing I can't have her, which thusly
causes me to long for her.

"OK, I'll get you this evening at seven thirty." I say not taking her no as a response.

"In any case, you don't have the foggiest idea where I reside."

"See you this evening." I say prior to hanging up on her.

"You asked her out?" He asks soon as the call closes. "Out on the town? The Steven asking a young lady out on the town. What's more, she isn't Linda? Amazing."

"Linda?" I rooster my head to check him out. What on earth does Linda have to do with this?

"Everybody definitely knows you and Linda will wind up together. Indeed, other than George, he says you will wind up alone and hopeless with a sexually transmitted disease or something to that effect."

Dismissing his side remarks I demand Stacy's location from him such he faltered prior to giving me.

Chapter 4

It was 7:32 and Stacy didn't actually annoy
looking external asI sounded the horn
tediously. I told her seven thirty,
for what reason am I actually staying here two
minutes
later. I escape the vehicle closing the
entryway behind me. I thump on her front
entryway and ring the doorbell a couple of
times.
"Who is it?" I heard on the opposite side of
the entryway.
"Steve. I answered.
The entryway opens up and she snorts
prior to feigning exacerbation at me, "How
did you get my location?" She overlays her
arms over her chest sitting tight for my
Response.
"I have my methodologies." My eyes lay on her
body. The red dress halting mid-thigh
also, embracing her hips. Her cleavage
crawling through the highest point of her dress.

Her rose smell filling my faculties as she
strolls past me to0 get to mny vehicle.
"You are a killjoy." She murmurs. I look
away from her body as she ventures into
the vehicle shutting the entryway behind her.
"I've been called more regrettable." She jeers
glancing back at me prior to getting into
the vehicle. I head over to the driver's seat,
driving from the front of her home.
"What is this?" She asks, resting her
head back on the seat, as she daydreamed
everything with the exception of the music.
"Al I Need' by Kodaline."
"I truly like this."
"It's pleasant isn't it?"
"Better believe it, it's something about music
like
this that I love."
"It resembles each tune takes you to a
better place, regardless of whether you never
been there it simply removes you.
It's unwinding and tranquil yet
musical and simply pleasant."
"Mm." She murmurs, I reach to turn the

sound system up similarly as, our fingers
brushing over one another's. She flushes
pulling her hand away andI turn up
the volume.
"Mm." She murmurs, I reach to turn the
sound system up similarly as, our fingers
brushing over one another's. She flushes
pulling her hand away andI turn up
the volume.
I appreciate seeing the impact I have on her
just by my hand contacting hers, I can't
hold back to see the impact I have on her
at the point when I'm within her. We sat
discreetly, the music being the main commotion
as I drove her to my #1 eatery.

How about we jump to the great part, I at last
brought the mental fortitude to ask Stacy out. I
was unable to bear not having her, whether it's
adoration or desire, I pine for her profoundly.

Steve's deal was extraordinarily acknowledged.
Obviously I need to get to know him
better. For what reason wouldn't any sensible

individual need t0 get to know him? He's
delightful to check out, amusing to converse
with,
snide, clever, snmart, coquettish, and
extremely insidious. He's the blend
of the ideal man, other than his grouchy
what's more, discourteous side. In any case,
there's consistently one
imperfection that makes an ideal man, no
longer appear to be awesome. To the extent that
we dated, Stacy continued to deny me to have a
vibe of her, I was constantly tortured by dreams
of her in my bed. I at long last fixed a meeting
with my primary care physician.
"Mr. Steve." He movements me to sit on
the couch before him.
"Dr. John." I protest plunking down
opposite him. "You truly need
to enlist another assistant or Dad, it's
getting feverish out there. The bizarre one
continues to attempt to converse with me."
"He isn't unusual Mr. Steve, he's simply
exceptionally open and communicates each and
every

thought he has, it doesn't make him
strange."
"No, he's strange." He's actual peculiar, you
recognize it clearly and the way he
talks. Something is off with that youngster.
He shot his tongue out to my ear and
murmured to me, I bet you didn't feel
me lick your ear.'I swear that youngster has a
few difficult issues happening in his
head.
"Somebody is getting doled out here
withina week or something like that." He tells
me.
"Trust it's a young lady and she's a hot blonde."
I quickly fantasize a charming blonde
with the shyest blameless grin, and
I tear her blamelessness from her in the
bathroom or behind her work area. I'm certain
the bizarre youngster wouldn't see any problems
the show.
Fuck, I just switched myself off adding
him into my little dream.
He watches me too intently now and then.
I glare, stopping before I speak, "I met

Somebody."
"OK, you meet a many individuals Mr.
Steve,Care to expand?"
"Dislike every other person." I glare.
She is totally not quite the same as
anybody I have at any point met. She's
bashful yet sure, dull yet so very
lively, pure yet lustful. She's
lovely to the eye and her fragrance is
appealing, alongside her exquisite style.
She remains in pastel hued skirts and
dresses and seldom wears pants.
Her edge is likewise an or more, surprising and
thick in the appropriate spots. She in a real sense
Doesn't have anything to be embarrassed about,
she is lovely.
"How long have you known her?"
"Just seven days."
"Have you laid down with her?"
"No."
"This makes her not the same as
every other person?"
"Indeed and negative."

"Indeed on the grounds that she would rather not rest

with you?" I gesture, "And negative?" He inquired

writing notes down in his cushion.

"Since not at all like any other person, I have this

desperate should associate with her."

"Is it safe to say that you are stricken by her Mr. Steve?"

"What?" I sneer. "Certainly not stricken,

Dr. John."

"OK, are you going to give me a name

to this young lady you're not stricken by?"

"Not this time." The last time I told him

about Linda, I was adequately moronic to

allow him to talk with her.

He looked for herself and asked her a

million and one inquiries regarding me.

She energetically offered him any responses to

the inquiries she knew the response to.

Then, at that point, she came examining me regarding

why I have a clinician. Obviously

I misled her, I told her I endure with
despondency. "You won't follow
this one as well."
He chuckles, "Don't rely on it Mr.
Steve. Are you actually having something very similar
dream?" He asked getting on point
once more.
"Consistently. Well aside from today."
"Really? What did you long for
today?"
"Nothing significant." I would rather not tell
him about this.
"It very well may be, what did you dream
about?"
"Me... what's more, Stacy." I rapidly add.
"Two inquiries." He expresses holding up his
list and center finger. "One, who is
Stacy? Also, two, what was going on
in your fantasy?"
"Dr. John, I truly don't think this is
of any significance. It sits around aimlessly
with any of my concerns."
"Your fantasies are one of your million

issues," he stops laughing at
supposed to be funny, "along these lines, answer
my
questions."
My telephone vibrates in my pocket, it's
Stacy. "I'll respond to one of your inquiries
before I accept this call. Pick carefully."
"What were you and Stacy doing in the
dream?"

"We were fucking, Dr. John." He glares
at me like he needs to Chasten me for
swearing once more and I sneer replying
the telephone.

Chapter 5

***I awakened needing to kiss you**. * I flush
perusing the message Steve sent me.
I was the principal thing he contemplated
when he awakened? He's actually thinking
about me. I can't conceal my grin.
Then, at that point, I called him in the parking
garage of my
school. He takes such a long time to answer I
thought it planned to go to voice message.
"Hi?" He replies.
"Howdy, it's Stacy."
"Indeed, I know. I truly do have this thing called
'guest ID,"
"Right." I laugh anxiously, "Do you
figure we can IOU on the supper
this evening?"
He stops briefly, "For what reason do
you need to drop?"
"I have a truly significant test
tomorrow, and on the off chance that I pass with
perhaps of the greatest score, I can get a paid

temporary job with one of the main five
clinician in one or the other Seattle or
Everett." I make sense of. "What's more, I truly
need to
study. This means a lot to me."
"I can assist you with considering." He says and
I
giggle, "Bring your books and so forth,
we will eat, then Il assistance you
study."
"You can't assist me with considering. You don't
actually
have a ton of familiarity with brain research."
"I'm a Shrewd man Stacy, I'm certain I can
sort it out." He is exceptionally shrewd yet he's
likewise very diverting. I surmise assuming that
I need
our relationship to develop then I can at
least allow him an opportunity. "So what do
you say?"
"Gracious, fine." I snort, "I will be there
this evening at seven."
"See you at seven." He answers. I get
the inclination he will be to a greater extent a

interruption then a partner.

Steve opens the entryway for myself and as
continuously he looks wonderful. He's wearing
a suit? "Continuously dressed so officially,
Steve?"
"I had as well." He murmurs grasping my hand
what's more, shutting the entryway behind me.
"Simply oblige it." He murmurs in
my ear. Oblige what? He takes
me into the lounge area. There was one dark
marble eating table with ten
white cowhide seats to coordinate. White
bloom filled containers finished the middle
of the table, just beneath the enormous precious
stone
crystal fixture. For a white, man,
his home is loaded up with it.
Three others were sat at the
eating table. A young fellow with blonde
hair absolutely not a chance close to past the age
of 25.
A wonderful brunette lady, and a
man with dim dark hair, most lkely

colored for a man of his age. This should be
Hayden's loved ones. They all look to such an
extent
the same, other than the various shades of
their hair.
"Stacy , this is my mum, Ashley. My
more youthful sibling, West, and my father,
Damain. Everybody, this is Stacy Greene.
I just acquainted a woman with my folks I can
barely handle it.
"Miss Greene." Damain remains from
the table arriving at his hand out to me.
He's wearing a rich dim fitted suit, a
white button down below, and a
dark, silver, and white striped tie. Much
unique in relation to steve's all dark suit.
"Goodness," I laughed peering down at my
hands. One was holding the pack with
my books and notes, and the other was
in Hayden's. Hayden discharges my right
hand and I shake Damain's hand. "Decent
to meet you Sir".
At the point when Steve's mom remains from
her seat, I stretch out my hand out to her.

Suddenly, she maneuvers me into a
warm hug. "Meeting you is wonderful,
Stacy."
"You, as well." She grins pleasantly at me.
She is truly spruced up as well. In a white
knee length trim dress, her hair up in a
amazing bun, and white pearls around
her neck and in her ears.
"Wow Steve, you neglected to specify
how lovely she is." West says
giggling. His English pronunciation is more
articulated than Steve's. Likely
since Steve lived here for longer.
West is dressed nonchalantly. Naval force
blue thin pants and a white Ramones
shirt. What is it with this family and
white?
Steve seems to be his mother more than
any other individual. "How long have both of
you
been dating?" She asked, a sweet grin
all over.
"Gracious, about seven days". answered Steve.
"That is no joke?" Damainn asks, and I

gesture, "What are you contemplating?"

"Im chipping away at getting my doctorate degree in Brain research. I's my last year."

"Truly? How old would you say you are?"

"23."

"Well

exceptionally youthful." Damainn mumbles disapprovingly. I'm as well youthful? For who?

"What drove you to need to study brain research?" Ashley inquired.

"My mom, she was a therapist."

"Was?" West inquired. his evebrows raised a score. I was trusting they wouldn't get on to that.

"Her mum is no longer with us." Steve says.

"Goodness," Ashley mumbles, feel sorry for surpassing her, "Please accept my apologies, love."

"Sorry to learn that." Damain says.

According to west, "It should be difficult to lose one of your folks. What happened to her?"

"My father said she was tanked driving
furthermore, got into a terrible fender bender."
They hushed up, Damian and Ashley
checking out at one another having a calm
discussion with their eyes.
By and by the table is calm and I
chosen to begin eating. Most of the way into
the calm dinner, I figured I'd discuss
Steve. "All of you should be truly glad
of Steve ." Ashley gestures grinning as she
checks her child out.
"What's there to be glad for?" Damon
answers scowling. Steve looks
down at his plate of food quiet, yet at the same
his
face is marginally tormented. I know steve
said his father was rarely fulfilled
with anything he did however this person is
unquenchable.
I grimace, "Mr. Damian, you're child in
extraordinarily shrewd and effective.
I have at no point ever met somebody
as sharp-witted as him. He holds the

information, brain, and educational encounters
past amazing. 26 years
old and he's accomplished considerably more
than my own dad at 55. An
proprietor of his own business with his
name on it? He's not working for
any other person, individuals are working for
him. Ordinarily at his age the main way
he'd get as much cash-flow as he
does is assuming that he had assumed control
over an as of now
well known privately-run company." I bluster,
not
thinking often about any destructive words that
may get away from my mouth at any given
second. "That's what this shocking spot
we are sitting in now, it has a place
to your child. What's more, also, he's
totally lovely and he takes care
of himself. There's a ton to be pleased with
Mr. Damian and it's a damn disgrace
that you are excessively dazed by envy to
see that."

"You're hanging around for a couple of moments
and you
think you know it all. You know
nothing about our family Miss Greene."
He snickers dryly, remaining from the
table he stomps out of the room. Ashley
sees me, grinning before she leaves
pursuing Damain.
Steve's demeanor is emotionless. I
haven't a sign with regards to how he is feeling.
"Im sorry Steve, I realize I shouldn't
have said that yet"
West giggles, "I love this young lady Stece
she's a manager."
Stevestands from the table taking
my hand once more, "We will be right back."
He tells West. I stand up from my seat and
follow behind him as he strolls
out of the room. I battle to keep up
with his huge strides as he drives me to
an alternate room. Delivering my hand
he turns on a faint light, shutting and
locking the swinging doors behind him.
"I couldn't say whether I ought to holler at

you or kiss you for conversing with my father
like that." says Steve.
"Please accept my apologies."
"Try not to be, child." Steve murmurs,
folding his long fingers over
my pig tail he pulls the flexible band
down, delivering my hair.
Good lord, Steve simply call me child,
what's more, it was so hot coming from him.
Most certainly something I would need to
hear again and again.
All that in me needs to bounce in
his arms and lose myself in him, however
I was the person who said I needed us
to take things slow. Perhaps I can make an
exemption for him.
Could he at any point determine what I was
thinking? I
wasn't focusing on what I was
doing. My eyes were shut, I desire to
God my lips weren't puckered.
"Except if you would rather not be simply
companions any longer?" He asked, a smidgen
of

trust in his voice.
"I don't have any idea what I need any longer."
I laugh turning away from his
delightful face.
"I understand what I need." He murmurs, his
thumb following across my base lip.
"Furthermore, what's that?"
I glance back at him, into his dim enlarged
eyes, and I need just to kiss him at the present
time. I need that,
I need to kiss him. "You."
My heart expands and I could no more
control myself as I press my lips on his
surprising him. He kisses me
back, running his warm tongue over
my lip. His tongue meets mine, and
they form to one another. Moving his
hand from my cheek to my midriff, he
pulls me nearer to him. Every last trace of
my body lighting. I never felt as such
with any other individual. It should be
something
about Steve.
I pull away gasping for much required

air, Steve leans his brow against
mine, his fingers on my thigh gradually
crawling up my dress. "Steve .." I
shake my head. I'm as yet not prepared for that.
"At the point when you're prepared." He murmurs,
kissing me once more. "In any case, we can do other
things."
His enormous hand cups the focal point of me
also, I pant, "In the event that you need to." He adds
discreetly.
"I need to." I mumble against his lips.
"OK then." He answers. I crash my
lips on his once more, my hands moving to
either sides of his face. I deliberately
buck my hips on his causing a cruel
moan to get away from his lips. He grins,
entertained and most likely turned on by my
activities.
Steve moved us onto one of the red
seats, me lying level on my back and
him sitting over me putting all his

weight kneeling down. "How have you
never been screwed? You're all
honest and fuckable, and with these
lips..." He runs his thumb across my
separated base lip, "Christ, everything turns
me on,"
"Indeed it does?"
"No doubt, that and the way that you're
bothered each time you're near
me."
"We should get you out of this dress, is that
right?"
He unfastens the main three buttons on
my dress, not turning away from my
face. His fingers move to the stitch of
my dress and he takes it off of my body,
I curve my back off of the seat to help
him get it off. He drops my dress on the
floor, his eyes now on my body.
"Stacy, you are fucking lovely. I can
see you like this the entire day." The way he
sees me alone is sufficient to make me
come unraveled. His eyes checking each
inch of my body, savoring all of my

bareness. Which just causes me to feel
incredibly timid. He moves so that he's
down on the ground. One hand moving from the
side of my head, he runs it down my
practically exposed body, making goosebumps
ascend on my skin. He admissions a sharp
breath as he slides his finger inside my undies,
focusing on my middle a
cadenced movement.
Gracious my. This feels better. In any case, how,
he's just scouring me? The muscles
within me grasping in the most
delightful style. Inclining down he
kisses me, his fingers not halting their
developments. His other hand moves
to my bra, his forefinger snaring
around the middle blood of my bra,
lifting my bra up liberating my bosom.
Trailinga line of kisses from my lips
to my neck and from my neck to my
bosom he shuts his mouth around my
areola, sucking and prodding. I proved unable
stop the groans and expands as they
gotten away from my mouth. The blend of

both feel better.
He murmurs something that I proved unable
get, his breath fanning my bosom. I
as I feel his thumb stroking my clitoris
a similar time he delicately nibbles my
areola, pulling it with his teeth causing
it to stretch, my legs solidifying as a
result. Gracious god what's going on.
"Actually no, not yet, child." Steve pulls my
undies down my thighs a little with
his free hand and when he embeds a
finger within me I nearly lose myself.
He gradually slides his finger out then, at that
point,
right back in, twisting and orbiting it
around and around. He does this sweet
anguishing torment again and again.
I couldn't say whether I can endure any more.
"Shows improvement over when you
do it?" What? Is it true that he is inquiring as to
whether I contact myself?
I open to my eyes to see steve's
expanded eyes with a slight ring of child
blue, gazing down at me. "I don't." I

murmur. I scarcely perceive my own
voice, it's so low bound with desire and
want.
"You don't for a moment even touch yourself?"
He asked, his eyebrows brought up in
wonder. Then he grins, "So
fucking honest."
Once more, there's that feeling. The
pressure works in my stomach and
my legs start hardening once more. Hayden
murmurs something against my mouth,
furthermore, I go to pieces on his hand,
"Gracious
Steve. " I groan, my body spiraling crazy.
He eliminates his finger from me, "How
was that?" Steve remains from the
sofa, leaving and returning
with a napkin.
"Astonishing." I answer enthusiastically. I have
never felt better. It was unbelievable.
He wipes his hand off giving me the
napkin next. I suppose I should
clear off with this. I do as such. Standing
from the sofa, I pull my undies back

up and fix my bra. My breathing has
however to get back to business as usual and my
heart is
hammering right out of my chest.
At the point when I head back in the other
direction Steve
holds my dress out before me,
"What was that?" "What?"
"On your back, pivot." He arranges
while he turns me around, my back
confronting him. "You have a tattoo?"
"No doubt, I got it when I previously turned
eighteen. My closest companion, Cindy
constrained me to get it." Steve runs
his hand over the tattoo simply above
the belt on my undies. Cindy
needed a tattoo however didn't have any desire
to do
it alone so she requested that I get one
with her. I didn't have the foggiest idea what to
get
also, I needed nothing too large or
recognizable, so I gota life line that goes
into a heart on my lower back.

"I like it." He presses a kiss on my shoulder.
I head back in the other direction taking the dress
from him and slipping it back on. "I
figure I ought to apologize to your father. I
truly crossed a line, I was simply furious
for you."I say fastening the highest point of my
dress.
"As you wish." He grasps my hand
driving me to the entryway.
I halt abruptly, "Stand by, shouldn't something
be said about
you? You need nothing in
return?"
"For the first time ever," he grins at me, "Im OK.
In any case, you owe me one day." Opening
the entryway he leads us back to the eating
room.

Chapter 6

Ashley and Damain were back in the
lounge area, and West was still in
there. I keep thinking about whether they were
sitting tight for
long. The plates of food are gone, and
they are currently drinking chilled wine.
I understand how we both should look
returning into this room. Pink
cheeks, disheveled apparel, rumpled
hair, and an ear parting smile. Yet, I
welcome the look since I feel perfect.
"Wine?" Steve asked getting
one of the glasses. I shake my head
no, plunking down once more. Hayden stands
behind me resting up against the seat
tasting on his wine.
"Mr. Damian, I truly need to apologize
for whatI said before. I was way out
of line. I let my sentiments outdo
me." It was exceptionally amateurish of me,
if I have any desire to be a clinician I need to
set my own sentiments to the side.

"You were off the mark," He tells me. "'In any case
you were right, at certain parts."
Steve stifles, nearly spitting his
wine out on my head. "She was?" He
asked a similar time I inquire, "I was?"
"Definitely." He murmurs. I'm more blissful
for the disclosure that Hayden is about
to get more so than the way that I
was correct.
"Steve do you have any idea about what amount
of time it required
me to get to where I'm currently? 21 years. I
took care of business four,
just about five years after you were conceived.
I couldn't say whether you recollect the days
where we had no food other than beans
what's more, toast. We smashed regular water,
our
lights were out three to five days out
of each and every month. Your mum worked
as a server while I sat on my arse
watching you. I needed to be enormous, I
needed to be rich so I can deal with

my family like a genuine man ought to. What's more,
with your mum's assistance, we got to where
we are presently." He grasps Ashley's hand,
giving it a light crush.
"I knew I maintained that you should be better
than me. That is the reason I pushed you so
hard constantly." He proceeds,
"However, when you really turned out to be better
than me, I was unable to deal with it. From the
outset, I was pushing you since I as a matter of fact
needed great for you, however at that point I pushed
you harder in light of the fact that I was furious with
you. Steve, I reached the place where
I begrudged you. You were precisely who
I needed to be. Also, I was unable to take
it. That is the reason I constrained you to come
here, to the States. I didn't need you. I
required you far away from me."
Ashley wipes the stack of her eyes,

Damain wipes away at his eyes, and
Ashley remains behind me unfeeling.
I take a gander at West, and he flags that we
ought to leave. I gesture remaining from my
seat. West strolls towards the entryway,
holding it open for me.
Steve lifts his head up halting me,
"Where are you going?"
"Im going to stand apart there with
West." I murmur to him. "Sick leave
you folks to talk."
"Much thanks to you." He murmurs, kissing my
brow and I leave the room with
West rests up against the wall his arms
collapsed over his chest, "Do you like him?"
"I don't actually realize him all around ok.
I mean he's hot as damnation and that's what I
like.
Furthermore, I like the prospect of him, however
I
don't have any acquaintance with him." I reply.
"Well you know significantly more now." He
laughs. Definitely, I am familiar with his loved
ones

life, yet I need to find out about
Steve himself.
"Better believe it, I surmise so." I mumble.
"You very much like the sex isn't that right?
Somebody to fuck readily available."
What? I nearly stifled on air when he
said this.
"No, we haven't ever"
"Truly? You didn't screw him yet? What
is it true or not that you are hanging tight for?"
"Im holding on to have intercourse with
Somebody who loves me."
"Oh my goodness, you're not kidding." He puts
a hand over his mouth to stop himself
from giggling. "What have you gotten
yourself into Steve?" He says nearly
softly.
"What do you and Steve do together?
Like you simply seem as though you'll be great
in
bed and tragically I've heard how Hayden
is, however since you're not fucking, what
precisely are you doing?" He murmurs,

shaking his head like he can't get a handle on
what he's talking about.
"We just truly talk." I answer his
question attempting to overlook everything
else he said.
"What's more, you're ready to satisfy all of his
he stops looking for the right word,
"indeed, his necessities?"
"His requirements?" I shake my head, having
no hint concerning what's going on with him
talking.
He scowls, "Sex, Stacy, It's what he lives
also, relaxes.'"
"Isn't it like that for everybody?"
"His aim for it makes
him contrast from every other person." He
answers discreetly as the entryway opens
once more.
Steve, Ashley, and Damain step out
of the room. What in all actuality does West
mean
by that? Steve needs sex? I'm so
befuddled. Steve snakes his arm
around my midsection, "you prepared to study?"

"Sure." However I don't think Sick be capable
to center.
"Stacy," Ashley makes some noise, "it was
wonderful
meeting you."
"You are leaving as of now?"
"They have an inn in the city." Steve
states, Ashley gesturing.
"Goodness, well I desire to see you all soon."
"Best of luck on your test Stacy. You'll
make an extraordinary clinician one day."
Damain mumbles.
"Much thanks to you."
"I'll walk you folks out." Steve says,
dropping his arm from my midsection.

…

Steve read over my notes and
asked me inquiries he believed were
significant, he diverted me at some
focuses yet generally he was
reprimanding me to remain on track.
"Goodness, this should be significant." He
murmurs while filtering my notes.

"You have it gazed like your notes on orientation and sexuality and mental messes." He said.
What is the
main difference between a habit and an addiction?"
I pause, thinking back to the lesson on addictions. "Oh, this was one of my favorite topics to discuss in this Course."
"You said that about everything." He chuckles.
I roll my eyes at him before answering his question. "A habit is a behavior pattern developed by frequent repetition of a certain act over and over to the point where the brain starts to do the act automatically. While an addiction is..."I elongate the s in order to think of the correct definition of the word. "It's a compulsive need of a certain thing or substance to the body." I continue.
"Do they have control over their habits

or addictions?" He asked quietly.
"The addiction has complete control
over the person and the person has control over
their habit or habits."
"How do you tell the difference
between habits and addictions?"
"Simple. Ask yourself can you live
without it. If you skip one day, and you
start to have withdrawal effects, it is an
addiction. If not, it's a habit."
Steve sets my notebook down, "Are
you sure habits and addictions aren't
the same?"
"Im positive they're not the same,
Steve. They're very similar though. A
habit can easily become an addiction
but a habit can be controlled or
modified while addictions can't
be controlled and they require professional help
for modification."
"Okay, we will go over that then." He
flips through pages looking for that
topic.
"Let's not." I murmur, sliding the book

from hinm to myself and closing it, "We can take a break."

"Well, sadly for you, you're a college student, who is actually going to study so she can get this internship. The one she was so excited about she tried to bail on my dinner. You're just going to suffer like I have to." He adds.

"Suffer?" I ask.

"Yes." He mutters.

"With what?"

"Waiting."

"Why are you waiting?"

"I want nothing more than to be inside of you and to feel you around me. And I'm suffering because you friend zoned me and you are a fucking tease. You don't make it easy for me to wait."

My breath gets caught in my throat and I am flushed bight crimson. Whenever he says things like this I never have a clue what to respond.

"I want to fuck you right now, and in order to avoid that, I need to be distracted. Please Stacy, study." Steve picks up the notebook again, flipping through the pages. And I thought I wasn't going to be able to focus before.

Chapter 7

My mind wanders to last night. I got somewhere
new with Stacy, my father's revelation,
spending my night helping Stacy study,
telling her how I actually felt. I wonder
idly if she finished her exam by now
and how it went. I spent my entire
morning, waiting to know how she'd
Thinking of you. How's the exam? I texted
her.

Trying to focus on work my receptionist walks
in, "The printer is down at the moment
sir, but Fredrick is already on it. Also,
Mr. Steve, you had a call during your
meeting but I didn't want to interrupt
So I took a message."
"Who was the call from?" I ask.
"It was a call from Stacy Greene, she
said she wanted to say thank you for
helping her study" She tells me
dropping a note on my desk.

"The next time Stacy Greene calls me
bring me the phone, it doesn't matter
what I'm doing at the moment."
"Yes, sir."
"That's all." I dismiss her and she nods.

Stacy

"You have an hour and ten minutes
to begin section one of your exam.
You may begin now." Oh shit, I got
distracted. I open the exam booklet
looking at question one.

**1. The painful experience associated
with the termination of an addictive
substance is known as**

Oh, this is going to be so easy. I finished
the one hundred multiple choice
questions with ten minutes to spare.
But for the two free-response questions
on the section two exam, I used all of
the fifty minutes I had. I was finally
done. Luckily, I was able to focus on it,
no thoughts of Steve or last night.
I shut my phone back on as I sat in

my car, in the parking lot. Speaking of
Steve. He texted me asking how my
exam went. I decided to call him to say
thanks instead of texting. "Mr. Steve
phone." I hear a woman say into the
phone.
"Oh...um hi, can I speak to Steve?"
"Mr. Steve is in a meeting at the
moment. Would you like to leave a
message?"
"Um sure, just tell him Stacy Greene
said thank you for helping me study
and I want to" I cut myself off,
"Never mind, just tell him I said thank you.
"Of course, I will give him the message
as soon as his meeting is over."
"Thank you."
"Have a nice day Miss Greene."
"You, too." I mutter ending the call.

...

We accepted our grades, and
luckly for me I was one of the five
understudies with the most noteworthy grades. I

gotten 147 out ofa conceivable 150
focuses.
Derek had the most noteworthy score with the
wonderful 150 score, then Renee with 148,
then, at that point, me, then Ryan and Hazel tied
with 146. We were each given a sheet
of paper with a name, a location, and
a period. The name of the specialist who
picked us to be their understudy, the location
of the structure, and the time we have
to be there each day.
As blissful as I'm to get the entry level position,
I really wanted to consider Steve. I
want to call him and fill him in about
the news yet I can't. I haven't spoken
to him Three days ago. I
Ignore his calls in general and his messages.
It's truly difficult to do in light of the fact that
Steve
is exceptionally constant and I miss being
around him and being in his organization,
be that as it may, I won't be another of his
resting mates. I'm superior to that.

I fixed the buttons of my shirt and
thrown it off of my shoulders. Curving
my back and bringing down my arms was
an irritated endeavor to get the shirt to fall
off, however because of the static it didn't. It
then, at that point, required the substitute choice,
for
me to raise and lower my shoulders to
release its hold. The shirt in the long run
fell between my back and the seat,
then I throw it to the side where my jeans
lie. "Steve, it's your arrangement and stop
expanding."
"Im not expanding, Stacy, Radiating.
perhaps. Sneering... conceivably. However
certainly not expanding. Also, assuming that I
was
expanding, which I'm not, I would have a
responsible motivation to expand."
Steve was certainly staring at ny
bosom, and however he attempted to deny
it with his words, his activities showed
in any case. He was down to his
pants and fighters, while I on the other

hand, was exclusively in my underpants.
The following round could turn out to be very
fascinating, it is possible that I planned to lose
my bra or Steve planned to lose his
pants. He at long last managed the cards,
taking a gander at the cards in my grasp, I throw
three of the cards in the
table, "Sick take three."
"Sick stay with what I have." Steve
answered, sliding three new cards my
way.
Rearranging the cards around in my grasp
I murmur, "Not really awful." Dropping three
Sovereigns on the table, I hang tight for Steve
to drop his cards or to overlap.
"Sorry." He deviously answers, laying
a successively ten high straight on the
table. Fuck.
"Sure." I half grin at him as I reach
despite my good faith to unclasp my bra
lashes, the lashes relaxing around
my shoulders. I physically pull the
lashes down my arms and drop the
bra with the remainder of my garments. Sitting

erect in the seat, I mix and arrangement
the cards without checking Hayden out.
In the wake of orchestrating the cards in my
grasp,
I look up at him. His eyes were focused
with my bosom. Assuming this were some other
circumstance, I would've been humiliated
being stripped like this before Steve, yet I was
marginally stimulated.
"Get your cards Steve."
"Presently, I'm expanding." He expresses,
getting
his cards from the table. I left it alone
to keep down my merriment as I arranged the
cards in my grasp. His attention on the
game totally evaporated, his eyes
deflecting from his hands to my bosom
furthermore, back once more. "Sick take two."
"None for me," I sneer at him, giving
him two cards. "Try not to back off of me
Steve, I can deal with a misfortune." I tell
him, after his last hand, I don't know
how great his cards are. Being that I
was exclusively in my undies, Steve still

in his jeans and fighters, I realize I was
at a more serious gamble of losing. In my grasp
was three Rulers and two 8's, I trust my hand to
the point of dropping my cards on the
table.
"Fuck." Steve collapsed, dropping his
cards downwards on the table and
remaining to eliminate his jeans. Venturing
out of his jeans, my eyes travel to his
his tight dark fighters stressing against
his noticeable phallus. Presently I'm the
one who's vast. "If I didn't have the foggiest idea
about any
better Stacy, I would've said you were
scoffing at my crotch yet you would
never." Only humorousness in his tone.
"Plunk down and arrange the cards."
Sitting down and getting the
cards, he grins, "It's anybody's down
presently Miss Greene."

"That it is Mr. Steve".
Subsequent to managing the cards, he looks
through his hand moving in his seat

while organizing his cards. I was
watching him cautiously, searching for one
transfer ownership of that gave what was in his
hands, yet there was nothing. Steve
had a damn decent emotionless expression.
"Sick take
two." I drop two inconsequential cards in the
focal point of the table while Hayden gives
me two cards. "Hot damn." I murmur
to myself, adjusting the cards in my
hand.
"One for me." He says, dropping one
card to get another.
This was it...I drop my give over;
a Ace , king, Queen , Jack, and a 10 of
clubs. Steve's eyes enlarge before he
drops his cards face down on the table,
"Fuck!" He swears.
"I win!" I gloat joyfully.
"Okay, Stacy, what is it that you believe should
do
until the end of the evening?"
I stop briefly to cause it to appear
like I needed to ponder what I needed.

I previously decided when this
thought to play poker rung a bell. "I
believe that you should have sex with me."

Chapter 8

"Come here." I stand up from the seat
strolling around the table to get to him.
He grasps my hand standing up and maneuvers
me into him. I suck in a sharp
breath as he lifts me up his hands
around my thighs and conveys me into
the room, his lips tenderly going after
my neck.
Lying me down on the sleeping pad he
jumps on top of me, riding my lap.
"Do you know how long I have
needed this? How hard it is for me to
express no to you?" Clasping my hand with his
again he kisses every one of my knuckles,
"You can never take this second back
Stacy, are you totally certain this is
what you need?"
"Indeed." I murmur, hypnotized by his
magnificence and delicacy with me. He
remains from the bed, leaving the room,
at the point when he returns he's holding a foil
bundle close by. Hanging over me once more

he appended his lips to mine.
Sacred screw we're going. I'm
going to lose my virginity to Steve
in Las Vegas. I never envisioned this
happening yet at the present time, I wouldn't
need this differently. I need him,
no, to hell with that, I really want him. I really
want him as
much as he says he really wants me. My body
wants his touch, his lips, his fragrance, his
voice, him.
"Is it true that you are thinking again?"
"No. I Wwant this." I gesture my head as I
talk. "I need this with you."
He murmurs, "Would you say you are certain?"
I offer him my response by crashing my
lips on his, kissing him hard. In the event that I
get the
chance ponder what I'm going to
do, I most likely wouldn't make it happen. I lick
his
lower lip, pulling it between my teeth.
He moans, sliding his tongue in my
mouth, his tongue massing over mine

as his hands travel around my as of now
stripped body. Because of the game the
just thing of apparel being worn by the
the two of us were our clothing. "I want
to hear you say it."
"Im sure Steve." How frequently
do I need to express it for him to
comprehend this is what I need. He is
what I need.
The muscles within me holding
flavorfully as he hangs over me squeezing a line
of kisses from my lips,
down my bosom, his tongue flicking my
areola as he passes the region, then down
to my hips. He kisses my hip bone,
sucks it, then runs his warm tongue
over the hurting spot. He rehashes his
unbearable activities a couple of times
previously
moving over to the opposite side to do
precisely the same thing, his lips and his
tongue touching off every last trace of me. My
precarious fingers tangle through his hair,
pulling as he keeps making marks

on my hip bone.
Steve runs tongue across the
belt of my white underwear. I felt it
right down there, pulsating with
delight. My moxie prepared to escape from
its typical abstention, and arrive at its once again
level of desire. His cerulean eyes gaze pruriently
into mine as
his teeth catch the belt of my
undies hauling them down my thighs
what's more, my legs, and throwing them behind
him. Goodness fuck, that was hot.
Steve drifts over me in a push-
up position his erect fighter clad crotch
squeezing into my sex, "You're totally
That's what wonderful you know?"
"Gracious god no," I flush, my cheeks turning
a brilliant shade of red as I lay underneath
him totally stripped. For what reason did I need
this so awful, I am so humiliated right
presently.
He lies himself on one side set
up on his elbow. His eyes obscure and
he nibbles his lower lip as he drinks my

body in, his two fingers going from
my lips, down my jaw and neck, over
one of my bosom, past my navel, and
to my middle. I found it hard to relax
as his thumb strokes my clitoris and
he murmurs, "No, what do you mean
no? Where are your habits Stacy, I
praised you." If my psyche and
my body were associated I would've
feigned exacerbation at him. He kisses the
corner of my mouth, a whine
getting away from my lips as his fingers enter
my vagina, he moves them in and out, slow
then quick then, at that point, slow once more.
Staying aware of his beat, his lips
move from mine, following kisses from
my facial structure down to my neck, where he
sucks on my skin. The spot pounding
as he kisses it delicately to compensate for the
cruelty. "At the point when you take a gander at
these in
the mirror, I believe that you should bear in
mind
me." He says, his lips moving from my

neck to my collarbone. He sucks on my
skin there. I must cover
these tomorrow.
He keeps siphoning his fingers in
what's more, out of me as his lips come to my
bosom. His tongue flicks my areola, it
solidifying under his capable tongue. He
nibbles it tenderly pulling it with his teeth.
"Steve..."I half groan and half
whimper, his activities become quicker and
somewhat more unpleasant until I come.
Eliminating
his hand from me, he sits up on his
knees and my eyes travel to his dark
fighters, stressing against his lump.
His eyes dim and brimming with hunger,
Steve holds the parcel out in front
of me, "Would you like to put it on me
or then again would it be advisable for me I?" I
was occupied with expanding at his
enormous shaft once he took his fighters off.
It generally stunned me how his fighters
had the option to contain every last bit of him, it
moreover

stunned me that that was all going
to be within me. Good lord. I'm
unexpectedly scared.
I take it from him, tearing the parcel
open. I hold the condom out, gazing
at the dangerous elastic. I've won't ever put
a condom on somebody, heck, I've never
touched a genuine condom. At the point when
we were
more youthful my sweetheart attempted to show
me by
putting one on a banana, telling me
I want practice for when my ex and I
at last make it happen. I giggle at the idea.
"What's so entertaining?"
"Nothing." I excuse it, taking the
ancient history absolutely insane. My
fingers were shaking as I drew them
nearer to him. I've needed this for so
since a long time ago I met him, however I'm
having
inconvenience putting on his condom.
"It isn't so difficult, here." He takes my
hands nmoving them towards him.

At the point when he relinquishes my hands, I brush
my thumb over his tip, cleaning endlessly
the wetness there. He moans, "Fuck,
child, assuming you rehash that I'll screw you
without the condom."
Alright, I swallow. This isn't hard or
muddled. I ought to simply slide it on.
I want to believe that I don't break it. I follow
my nature and slide the condom dovwn his
hard skin. He gazes down at my hands,
sucking in a sharp breath. "Stacy, are
you sure you need this?"" He asks me
again once I moved my hands.
"Steve we previously made it this far,
I wouldn't stop this now." I reply,
carrying my lips to his. He answers
rapidly, kissing me gradually. His tongue
prodding mine as he lays me back on
the bed, situating himself between
my legs. Interweaving our fingers, he
moves them to the two sides of my head,
nailing me down on the bed.

"On the off chance that it harms just let me
know, alright?"
He kisses me delicately, brushing his nose
against my cheek. Such a sweet motion
for what might be said about's to occur.

I gestured, and shouted out as he gradually
pushes
his genital into me, my eyes screw
close and I wheeze in torment. This feels
bizarre and extremely, awkward.
Steve moves, "Ow," I chuckle at the
awkward torment.
"You alright?" He asked through gritted
teeth, gradually filling me. However, i gesture,
I was everything except. He remains still and
when I take in his full length he inquired,
"Might I at any point move?"
"No doubt." I mumble, my voice weak, and
he goodness at such a leisurely pace pulls out
and goes right
back in then stills.
"Once more?" He inquired. It fucking harms like
damnation andI simply need the awkward

agony to die down so I can partake in this second with him. I gesture as a tear rolls
down my cheeks. Once more, he moves and kisses me. "Fuck, that is no joke." He
moans. Assuming I were available I would've said something about being unique
then each of different ladies he's of all time been with, yet I couldn't in fact shape a
legitimate sentence.
My hands hold his back firmly, my nails mauling at his skin, as he push into
me, done halting to request my assent. The aggravation dying down as I observe
Steve, his eyes shut as he push in furthermore, out of me, his lips marginally
separated as he inhales intensely, his jaw gripped
showing his ideal facial structure, and his muscles agreement and pull against his
skin as he moves. I'm totally in wonderment of this man. "Are you... are you
alright?" He falters the inquiry. My hips probably meet his as he picks
up his speed, pushing quicker. My hands

move to his rowdy yet delicate hair pulling
what's more, he drives himself into me. He
brings down himself onto me and I quickly
append my lips to his own, then, at that point,
moving
to his collarbone. My lips kissing the
skin simply above it, prior to sucking on his
skin.
Iwas going to do it on his neck until I
recalled Steve could do without
love chomps or as he refers to them as
"proprietors
chomps" in light of the fact that to him, it's like
putting
a proprietorship on somebody's body. He
appreciates giving them however doesn't ever
need to get one. In any case, at this moment, he
is mine similarly as I'm his.

My body starts to solidify as Steve
keeps on pushing endlessly. I
interface my lips to his again Steve's
tongue darts out to my base lip and
I moan into his mouth. He smiles and

kisses me once more, our tongues investigating
the others, gulping every others
groans. "I am almost there, Baby." Steve
moans,
I'm not prepared for this to be finished,
other than the torment and distress felt in
the starting I am cherishing this. Waiting
was worth it, Steve is worth it.
Steve lips press to my earlobe before
biting it and I convulse around him
as I reach my climax. With a few final
thrust Steve follow suit, emptying
himself into the condom. "Oh fuck."
He breathes. He kisses me again, and I
wince as he slowly pulls out of me.
"Are you okay?" He asked me, lying
down beside me on the bed and
removing his condom and tossing in
the waste bin by the bed. I cover myself
with the sheet and Steve does the
same.
"Im great." I smile widely at him and
press my thighs together, an attempt to
rid the ache I felt there. Playing with

the top of the sheet I ask him, "What do
you have to do tomorrow?"
"I have some early morning meetings
scheduled for tomorrow." He answers,
his chest still heaving rapidly as he
tries to recollect his breath. "We can go
out for the night, if you'll be up for it."
"We will have to see how tomorrow
plays out." I smile meekly at him.
"Get some sleep Stacy, we can talk
about it tomorrow." He moves behind
me and pulls me into his embrace
wrapping his arm around me, I am
facing away from him. I hear him let
out a heavy sigh and he kisses the
spot just below my ear, "How are you
feeling?"
"Im good." I reply with my eyes closed.

Chapter 9

I was looking forward to going out to
the nightclub Steve's friend owns,
but I was anxious to know what
Steve had planned for right now.
Tentatively I take my dress off, my eyes
staying on the man standing behind
me, watching carefully as I undress.
"Now what?" My voice low and desire
stimulating deep inside of me.
"I must admit Stacy, I loved when you
put on a show for me." There's that
word; love. "Like when you touched
yourself in the bed. Do it again."
What? I flush. I can't do that. I was
entirely intoxicated, my thoughts and
judgments clouded. There's no way
I can touch myself knowing exactly what I'm
doing.
"Oh don't be coy now Stacy." He's
amused by my embarrassment. "If
you want, I can assist you in starting

yourself off." Steve offers.
With my lack of responses, Steve
steps towards me again using his leg
to push my feet further apart. Taking
in my tense and completely horrified
expression he moves my hair to one
side and kisses the exposed flesh in the
crook of my neck, his teeth grazing my
skin. Taking my hand in his, he closes
my hand with the exception of two
fingers; my index and middle finger.
"Tell me what helped get you off that
night?"
I shrug. Though I remember more than
I want or am willing to admit about
that night.
"Stacy, talk to me baby, what was it?
What was going through your mind?"
I flush again before I find it in me to
answer his question, "You."
"What about me?" He asked bringing
our hands to his lips. He kisses the pad
of my fingers. His eyes watching us in
the mirror. "What did you imagine?"

I can't talk about this with him. It's too
embarrassing now that I don't have a
drink in my system. "I imagined your
hands as my own." I answer quietly.
Catching me completely off guard he
sticks my fingers into his mouth and
sucks on my fingers coating them in
his saliva then releasing my fingers.
"You needed lubrication." He speaks his
voice thick with nothing but lust.
With one hand splayed across my belly
he uses the other to push my panties
aside and eases my own two fingers
inside of myself. My heart beating out
of my chest as he releases my hand
telling me to continue. I began to follow
the rhythm Steve usually did, but
it didn't feel as good as when Hayden
did it. I don't know how I managed
to get myself off last time when I feel
completely lost without his hand
guiding me. "You look sexy touching yourself."
Steve says kissing my back.
Using my own thumb he strokes my

clitoris diagonally, "That's right, baby,
do it again, curve your fingers." He tells
me, his eyes watching my hands move
between my legs. Steve commanding
me on what to do makes this all the
more titillating.
Unclasping my strapless bra, and
taking it off of me himself he takes
my free hand in his. He moves our
hands upwards to my breast making
me cup myself, guiding my fingers as
they stroke my nipples, causing them
to harden under my touch. I close my
eyes as I continue touching myself,
Steve's hand no longer guiding me.
"How good does it feel?"
"So good Steve." I moan, forcing
myself to think of my hands as
Steve's. It does feel good, and it's
arousing knowing Steveis watching
me and likes for me to do this. Opening
my eyesI look at him through the
mirror, "Can you do it too?"
If he's making me do this then I want

him to do it as well. I want to watch
him the way he's watching me. Steve
touching himself would be more
arousing than me touching myself.
"Do what?"
"Touch yourself."
"No, baby," he chuckles, "I don't
Pleasure mvself"
"Please Steve?" I need him, and
watching him would surely help me
find my release.
He takes a step beside me palming
himself over his pants, "Ill only do
this for you baby, just this once." He
tells me unzipping his pants, wrapping
his hand around his hard impressive
length. If he doesn't touch himself
usually, no one would be able to tell.
He's so confident when it comes to
anything sex related, it's something I
want to learn from himn. I watch in awe
of him, his hand moving faster and
faster, pumping himself harder.
My body begins to stiffen, signaling

just how close I am. "I won't last long watching
you." Steve groans causing
myself to moan. "You don't know how
attractive you look like this. Look
at yourself, look how beautiful and
flawless you are."
I look at myself instead of him. My
cheeks were flushed scarlet, my hand
still groping my breast while the other
still moves between my legs. I moan
his name as I find my release from my
own doing. Steve follow suits aiming
at my belly after watching me come
undone on my own fingers.
I gasp as his undoing hits my bare
abdomen, Steve finding himself
amusing. "Steve," I whine. Why
on earth would he find this funny?
The moment we just shared was so arousing, so
erotic, then he goes and
does this.
"I needed somewhere to aim." He
chuckles kissing my lips. He takes the
hand towel from the rack and cleans

my stomach off, along with my own
hand. "Better?"
"Yes, thank you."
"Alright, let's go to this nightclub."
Steve changes to his casual black
jeans and black t-shirt, throwing on
a black bikers jacket before we left
the house.

The club is called Slotted. The interior was
totally white; the padded couches,
the bar counter and stools, the marble
floor, and the walls, with various
shades of blue glaring lights
moving about. Crowds of individuals were
all over, Steve grasped my hand
driving us towards the celebrity segment.
The main thing we're given is a shot
glass loaded up with an unmistakable fluid a cut
lime
holding tight the cup. Taking the lime
off, I swallow down the beverage, truth be told
rapidly, flinching as the consuming liquor

slid down my throat. A man gets
Steve and I and strolls towards us,
an entertained smile put all over.
"You said you would have been here
at 8:30, you're never one to be late for anything."
"Something came up." Steve grins.
"I expect it has something to do with
the shapely goddess to one side."
His eyes don't leave my body while he
talks. "You have neglected to present us.
I'm Eric Doorman."
"Stacy Greene." He makes a stride towards
me and inclines toward me, Steve puts a
hand out preventing him from whatever
he was going to do. Eric checks out
Steve and steve shakes his head
'no'. "You're not ready to share this
one?" Offer?
"Haven't arrived for that this time Eric".
simply maintain that Stacy should have a
goodbye
out." What are they referring to?
A youthful female strolls over radiating,
"Steve, it's so great to see you once more!"

I was tossed when she snatches all things considered
side of his head and kisses him on
the lips. My jaw dropped to my feet
at the point when he kissed her back. What the
for hell's sake? Pulling away from him she murmurs
gratefully, "]ust like bygone eras."
Turning away her regard for me she eyes
me all over hypothetically, "You're
exceptionally lovely." She applauds. "Im
Juliet Doorman, you are?" Eric's better half?
I was unable to conceal the shock and disarray
in my voice as I spoke, "Stacy Greene."
Shocking me totally she
kisses me, her hands on my midsection. I
didn't have the foggiest idea what to do, Steve didn't
stop her like he halted her significant other. I
can't help thinking about why that is. As awkward
as this made me, I set my sentiments to the side
what's more, cup either side of her face kissing
her. She sneers breaking the kiss first. I

investigate at a sneering Steve and he
simply shrugs getting us another beverage.
I needed to get some information about the
trade among us and the Watchmen
in any case, I never carved out the perfect open
door as they
remained with us the whole evening. Getting
us a beverage after another beverage, talking
with us, snickering with us. Until I neglected
about it all together. Steve held me
near him, scowling at Eric and
Juliet each time they contacted any piece of me,
regardless of whether it was only my hand.
My ongoing brain outline was to get on
the dance floor. "I will go dance."
I swallow down one more shot and stand
to get to the dance floor.
"Sick watch you from here." He says to
me, and watch he did, each development
I made his eyes remained on me. His
look from across the room was not
just satisfying yet in addition erotic. His
base lip between his teeth, his eyes
dim and scoffing into mine. I made due

to maintain eye contact with him while I moved
ignobly on the floor.
I dance alone watching him watch me,
my hands investigating my dressed body, I
believe he should go along with me. I get some
distance from him and dance.
I felt his hands creep around my
abdomen, just they weren't Steve's.
They were bonier and more modest than
his. I go to confront the more bizarre behind
them, he grins down at me his brown
eyes fixed with mine. The blue lights
moving around his face as he moves his
hips into me. I drive myself away from
him however he doesn't permit it, holding my
midsection more tight. "Don't bother me." I push
against him to free myself.
"Try not to quit moving for my sake," He
slurs, "you looked delightful and desolate
moving without anyone else."
I believed that Steve should hit the dance floor
with me
not a total more peculiar who doesn't have the
respectability to request to move

yet rather improperly contacts
whomever he satisfies. I investigate
where Steve was sat yet he was no
longer there. I push against him once more,
"Relinquish me." I whimper.
"Unwind, I won't hurt you, I just
need to move." He tells me haughtily.
Quickly a seething Steve
drives the person away from me sending
him into a gathering who moan
irritated with the person for knocking
into them. I slap a hand over my mouth
to prevent myself from chuckling as Steve
tosses a weighty catastrophe for the folks jaw.
"What on God's green earth?" He yells holding
onto his jaw.
Steve scowls at him, his annoyance
unmistakable, "Keep your filthy hands off
of my young lady."
Steve goes to me his bleak
articulation mellowing, his finger
strokes my cheek, "Would you say you are
alright?"
"Are you?" I betray

him with a delicate laugh. I clutch his
wide strong lower arms, fixing my
lips to his. "Much thanks to you."
"I need to safeguard what's mine."

Steve and I left Vegas at 4 in the
morning and landed 6:15, I had an
hour in excess before I needed to make a beeline
for
the workplace. I picked a new shower,
bunches of water, and an ibuprofen to
cheer myself up during my
day. I didn't get a lot or scarcely any
rest the previous evening and I tanked more than
I ought to have been. It's absurd the number of
drinks Ive had since I met Steve. I
went from not drinking by any stretch of the
imagination to having
a drinks consistently.

Chapter 10

Six additional days have passed I still
haven't heard from Steve by any stretch of the
imagination.
The primary day, I had work to occupy me
from my viewpoints of him during the
day and when I returned home Rule was
there to keep me involved. We went
shopping, we spoke for a really long time about
our old recollections as we glanced through
photograph collections drinking wine. I didn't
actually
invest an excessive amount of energy pondering
him, I forged ahead with my day. As it were
a couple of times I pondered; what is he
doing at present, how is he, where is he.
The subsequent day, I continued to check my
telephone. I figured he would simply call
or on the other hand even text me. I didn't have a
lot of opportunity to be on the telephone while I
was
working, yet without a doubt when I was

on mid-day break and when I had a
free second, I was checking my
telephone for a missed call. Yet, to my
disillusionment there was rarely a
missed call from him. By the time I
returned home, my telephone didn't leave my
hand briefly and I hopped each
time my telephone hummed. I went from
really looking at my telephone consistently to
consistently until I nodded off.
The third day, I cried. I cried so fucking
hard. The fact that he didn't call me makes me
hurt. I
think the truth hit me this day. I knew
he won't get back to me. I was
left asking 'Is there any valid reason why he
won't call me?"
"What did I foul up?' I even made up
a few responses. Perhaps I was terrible to the
point that he believes nothing should do with me
also, he at no point ever needs to see me in the
future.
Perhaps he's so occupied with work that

he lacks the capacity to deal with any other
person.
Perhaps he simply could do without me and I
was
simply one more young lady for him to fuck. No
doubt,
the last response made me cry harder. I
wept well into the night.
The fourth day, it was Rule's last day,
she let me know she would have rather not left
me in my present status. I told her I
was fine however I was everything except.
The moment she left to go to the air terminal
I cried more. I felt objectified and like the
one thing I never needed to be; a sex
toy. I broke my guarantee to my mom,
Steve wasn't the most ideal one for me. I looked
past all of things he did to show me
that he wasn't the one due to my affections for
him. I truly like him and it
harms that he doesn't feel the same way
about me. I could never wish to take
my most memorable time with him away, I
simply wish

it finished in an unexpected way. I wish he felt the

same way about me as I did him.

The fifth day, I was in rage. I didn't really

need a call from him. I called

him a butt hole and needed nothing to

do with him. He saw no point in calling

me or coming to see me. He couldn't have cared less

about me. He screwed me over. What

kind of individual rests no, screws a young lady

then at no point ever converses with her in the future? Then

it hit me. Steven is this sort

of individual. He screws a young lady and never

addresses her once more. He doesn't rest

with them, he screws them. That is what

he told me. This is the point at which I got angrier

since I understood I was a blockhead. In any case

I resented myself more than with

him. I let him do this to me. He inquired

me so often on the off chance that I was certain
and I
said OK. He realized he planned to leave
me before he even screwed me. I just
allowed him to screw me over.
What's more, today, today is the 6th day. I still
haven't heard from him. I simply care about
replies. How could he do this to
somebody? I accept, after everything
that occurred, the least he can accomplish for
me is offer me a few responses. Really I don't
need to express farewell without knowing
precisely why I'm expressing farewell to him.
I thump gently on the entryway, still
choosing if I ought to simply leave or remain. If
I leave, I will not get any of the responses I'm
searching for. Be that as it may, on the off
chance that I stay, I stress
that I'll fall into another of his
traps.
The entryway opens yet rather than seeing
Steve, I was welcomed by the young lady from
one of
Steve's party. What is she doing here

with Steve?
Well now I know why Steve has
never got back to me. He's distracted
with this skank, Linda. I couldn't actually say
whether
she's a skank, however I truly could do without
her so
that is the very thing I will call her for the time
being. Prostitute
disgracing at its best.
"Greetings, Stacy right?"
"Indeed, you're Linda?"
"Steve discusses me to you as well
huh? He's been discussing you non-
stop since he initially met you at the bar. I
likely have a deep understanding of you."
She says giggling. Steve converses with her
about me?
"He has?"
"Yes, and I won't lie, it is so
irritating. Would you like to come in?
Steve is in the shower." She moves
aside and I stroll past her going into the
house. Assuming that Steve is in the shower he

should not know I'm here, and that implies
Linda was the person who gave the acceptable
for
While I have a couple of moments previously
he emerges from the shower I need to question
her and get so a lot
data from her as I can. She sits
down on the lounge chair and taps the seat
close to her, flagging me to sit. At the point
when I
do, she begins talking first.
"I revere your skirt, did you wear that
intentionally?"
"Deliberately?" I shake my head not
understanding what she implied.
"You know, Steve loves when
young ladies wear skirts." She says as though
I should know that kind of
data. "You didn't wear that for
him?"
"No, I didn't."

"Goodness," she giggles, "so you simply do
what

he loves easily? He used to
need to tell me before I came over that
I'd need to put on a skirt. Skirts were
never actually my thing, I'm even more a
thin pants sort of young lady."
Staying here before Linda, talking
with her about Steve, it was in this
second I came to the realization I
am very desirous of her. I begrudged
her for her lovely appearance, her
stunning casing, her set of experiences with
Steve.
She had him while I was let be
crying since I needed him. She
knows such a huge amount about him, I scarcely
have a ton of insight into him. She has him
the way I need him.
"I wear pants every so often, generally I wear
skirts or dresses." I answer,
setting my desire to the side, coming
with her current discussion.
"That is something else he enjoys young ladies
wearing. Dresses. He says it's simple
access or no big deal either way. I just told him,

he's fortunate he gets me consistently. If he
needs somebody wearing those to go
find another person, and that is precisely
what he did." She says chuckling, however I'm
not finding this amusing. Is Linda like his
screw pal or something like that... also, in the
event that she
is, what is she doing here at this point?
"You're precisely very thing he needs Stacy. "
She mumbles with an unpleasant chuckle
followed by a grimace. "Not me.
I'm not what Stacy needs, he simply needed me
for one thing and I
enthusiastically gave it to him. That is the reason
I'm
here, to stand up to him about the untruths he
taken care of me since I met him.
I must be cautious with him. He
knows precisely very thing to say and precisely
when to say it. He knows where and
how delicate to contact me to ploy me back
to him. What's more, I will capitulate to his
words
what's more, his touch.

I drive myself to get some information about her
also, Steve. Finding a solution
from her would without a doubt impact my
discussion with Steve at whatever point
he escaped the shower. "Are you and
Steve Sleeping together?" I ask her.
She opens her mouth to talk however gets
disturbed. God damn it, she was about
to offer me a response. "Linda, would it be
advisable for us we…
-Stacy?" Stevs quits strolling down
the means as he sees me and checks out
me stunned.
I really wanted to see he was as it were
covered by a white towel, which hung
mouthwateringly low around his v waist.
Showing his delightfully characterized V line,
what's more, the line of hair from his maritime.
His
body shimmering with water drops, his
hair dull, wet and tacky from being
washed. Amazing. I'm presumably slobbering
at the sight, I ought to turn away. However, I
can't.

Since that Sunday night in Vegas, I have
been needing him, his lips, his fingers,
his shaft, my body wanted all aspects of him.
That Saturday night, when I
deliberately gave him my goodness, I got
a preference for something so prurient, so
exotically customary and I was left with
a craving for him.
"What are you doing here?"
"I-" This will be diverting. I
drive myself to see his face, "I came
here to find solutions."
"Replies?"
"Indeed, replies, I took a stab at giving you time
also, space so I didn't need to be one
of those young ladies, however I'm worn out on
pausing
Steve." I say, my eyes falling back to
his impeccably conditioned body.
"Okay...I can answer your questions."
"First," however much it torments me to say
this, "Im going to require you to put some
garments on, it's extremely challenging for me to
center around the thing I'm attempting to say."

My words immediately causing the corner
of his lips eccentricity into a harsh and
profoundly enchanting sneer. He starts to
stroll back up the moves toward get to his
room when Lina makes some noise, "Steve,
I will take off so you all can
um... talk?"
"Okay, I'l see you around." He says
strolling off.
She snatches every last bit of her things, "It was
truly decent seeing you again Alice."
Ijust grinned at her before she left,
abandoning me in the room. She
never responded to my inquiry.
"What did you need replies to?"
Steve asked me, hopping directly into
the discussion once he gets down
the means. Steve returned wearing
dark pants and he was throwing a
dark shirt over his head.
"I needed to know why you haven't
called."
"I was occupied." He shrugs.

"Occupied with Linda? Or then again occupied with attempting to
stay away from me? I stood by so lengthy for you
Steven. I let you take my virginity and
you direct this large number of sentiments toward me like I'm yours then, at that point, leave me sitting tight for you for
all the more then seven days, and all you need to say for yourself would you say you is were occupied? Did
you just spend time with me so you can
screw me, then, at that point, you throw me to the side like
you do all the others? Am Ijust
one more young lady you fucked?"I stood up from the love seat, flying off the handle with him
once more. I was standing near him, however too far off to contact him.
"It's more muddled than that, Stacy. "
"Why is it so muddled
Steve? It is possible that you like me or you don't. You utilized me or you didn't." He

shakes his head, not uttering a word.
"You're such a weakling, you can't even
come clean with me. You use I was occupied' as
a reason. I gave you such an individual
also, sacrosanct thing, Steve you took it
also, left never to return. I think I at
least merit a genuine explanation with regards to
why
you concluded you needed your space.
You may not know this
about me Steve, but I'm the type of
girl that needs reasons why I'm getting
fucked over."
"Im a coward?" He asks, sounding
angry or hurt. Or maybe both.
"Yes, that's what I said."
"Fine, you want to know the real
reason I left and never called?" He
raises his voice a little.
Of course I do! That's the reason I'm here!
"Yes, please, do tell me." I match his
voice.
"I haven't called because you confuse
the fuck out of me and I can't seem to

think straight when I'm around you.
Stacy, you make me want to do things I
promised myself I'd never do."
"What?" His confession left me
confounded.
"Stacy, I'm falling for you. Deeply. And
that, scares the fuck out of me. When
we had sex, the feeling I got from it
was surreal and quixotic. Then you fell
asleep in my arm, Stacy, I didn't want
to move from that position I wanted to lay there
with you forever. The entire
weekend brought to my attention my
affinity for you. Not just for sexual
pleasure but in general, Stacy. I have
emotions for you that no amount of
words, complex or simple, can be
put into prospective to allow you to
understand what it is I'm feeling for
you."
All of my previous anger and sadness
with him over the past week dissolving
with every word that escaped his lips.
My heart fluttered, but a small part

of me didn't know if he was actually
telling the truth. "Steve please don't
lie to me or say things you think I want
to hear. I just want the truth."
"For once baby, I'm being honest with the both
of us."
He sounds so sincere, but that small
part of me won't stop thinking this is
just a trick for him to get in my pants
again.
"I want you, in a way I have
never wanted anyone else. So maybe I
am a coward, but that's because I don't
know how to deal with these feelings.
I didn't know what it was until I spent
these days away from you and every
second of my day was spent thinking
about you. I was trying to figure this
shit out. I'm sorry." He stands in front
of me, cupping my face, his thumb
tracing my lower lip, "Do you forgive
me?"
My heart was beating out of my chest,
and I wanted to kiss him and tell him I

forgive him, but that's way too easy.
"You don't believe me?" He asked
looking in my eyes, his blue eyes
searching my face for words I'm not
saying. He drops his thumb from my lip
to my chin.
"I want to Steve, but"
"Stacy, I wouldn't lie to you. Not
about this." He says cutting me off.
"I had a hard time being away from
you. Every second of my days, my
thoughts were consumed by you. I
tried to distract myself from you but if
I paused for even a second, my mind
was overtaken by inordinate thoughts of you.
The amount of hours I spent
thinking of you, dreaming of you is
unhealthy. Thinking of you kept me
up at night, I missed you being with
me, I missed hearing your voice, your
adorable giggle, your titillating moans
when I gratify you, feeling your lips
against mine." He mutters his thumb
tracing the outline of my lip, his eyes

darkening as he stares down at me. "I
had an insatiate yearning to have you
back with me Stacy."
"Im not just another girl you fucked?" I
asked, my voice quiet.
"Nothing like them." His voice soft, in
contrast his dark dilated pupils.
Steve is being so honest with me.
I take this opportunity to ask the
question that has been bugging me
since I walked in the door."Did you
sleep with Linda?"
"No, Stacy. I want you not her, she
knows that now."
"Okay."
"It won't happen again." He promises,
dipping his head down to mine
nuzzling his nose against mine. I wrap
my arms around his neck, pressing my
lips to his. Taking it slow and sweet.
Our tongues finding each others,
caressing, fondling the others. God,
I've missed him. Steve moves his
hand from my face down my back and

he flexes his hand over my behind squeezing it. I moan into his mouth.

"I have missed you so much." Steve says. "I've been going insane without you, baby."

"I missed you too, Steve." Oh no, I'm going to cry. I don't want to cry anymore. I nestle my face in his chest to hide my tears. I don't want him to see me cry.

"Baby, no, please don't cry. I'm sorry." He whispers his apology as he holds me tighter in his arms, only making me cry more. "Stacy please, I told you this would happen. I'm so sorry." He whispers again.

"Stay here with me tonight?" Steve asked after a while of us being in one another's arms.

"Okay." He lifts me off of his chest, attaching his lips to mine while apologizing again.

"Your lips are so soft when you cry." He frowns looking down at me, his fingers

wiping away at the tears staining my
cheeks. "I don't want to be the reason
behind your tears."
"Then don't be."
"I will try, baby. I promise."

Epilogue

And I found yet another addiction, Stacy.
She is my world.

Conclusion

Fix
This is the point in the recuperation where
the junkie attempts to fix themselves,
Furthermore, their lives.
This is where they get themselves back
on target. This is where Steve is presently,
or then again where he was attempting to be.
Development.
The last stage is obscure to Steve.
He hasn't had the option to arrive at this point,
however. Be that as it may, he knows with the
assistance of Dr.
John and Stacy, he can get to where
he should be. This is where he needs
to be, so he and Stacy can be blissful
together, and his dependence be an old,
revolting memory he won't ever need to
abide into at any point down the road.

www.ingramcontent.com/pod-product-compliance
Lightning Source LLC
Chambersburg PA
CBHW072054150726
47999CB00005B/1776